Our
Philadelphia

Jerry Irwin

Voyageur Press

Edited by Josh Leventhal
Printed in China

05   06   07   08   09   5   4   3   2   1

Library of Congress Cataloging-in-Publication Data
Irwin, Jerry.
  Our Philadelphia / Jerry Irwin.
    p. cm.
  ISBN 0-89658-697-9 (hardcover)
  1. Philadelphia (Pa.)—Pictorial works. 2. Philadelphia (Pa.)—Description and travel. I. Title.
  F158.37.I79 2005
  974.8'11'0222—dc22

                              2004028298

Published by Voyageur Press, Inc.
123 North Second Street, P.O. Box 338
Stillwater, MN 55082 U.S.A.
651-430-2210, fax 651-430-2211
books@voyageurpress.com
www.voyageurpress.com

Educators, fundraisers, premium and gift buyers, publicists, and marketing managers: Looking for creative products and new sales ideas? Voyageur Press books are available at special discounts when purchased in quantities, and special editions can be created to your specifications. For details contact the marketing department at 800-888-9653.

Page 1: *The city of Philadelphia spreads along the Delaware and Schuylkill Rivers in southeastern Pennsylvania with a blend of modern urban landscapes and centuries-old landmarks.*

Page 2: *A carriage ride around the Old City and Society Hill neighborhoods is a great way to explore our nation's history.*

Page 3: *"Love Park" at JFK Plaza has become a symbol of the City of Brotherly Love. Created by Robert Indiana in 1978, the sculpture sits across from City Hall in Center City. Its letters each stand twenty feet tall.*

Page 4: *Blooming annuals and perennials fill JFK Plaza as the stately City Hall looms large between modern office buildings.*

Page 5, top: *Elegant and pricey townhouses dot Philadelphia's fashionable Rittenhouse Square neighborhood. These homeowners came up with a creative solution to decorate their shared doorway.*

Page 5, bottom: *All thirty-nine signers of the United States Constitution, including Philadelphia's own Benjamin Franklin, are on life-size display in bronze at the National Constitution Center in Independence National Historic Park.*

Title page: *The city skyline reflects in the Schuylkill River at night, highlighting many of Philadelphia's most prominent landmarks: Boathouse Row, the Philadelphia Museum of Art, the PSFS Building, and City Hall.*

Title page inset: *The world's most famous cracked bell: the Liberty Bell.*

Facing page: *Philadelphia's Center City presents a contrast of modern glass-and-steel skyscrapers and classical brick-and-stone buildings.*

On the cover
Front cover: *Elfreth's Alley in the Old City.*
Back cover, counterclockwise from upper left:
Statue of state founder William Penn atop City Hall.
The fountain at Logan Square.
Piladelphia's skyline over the Delaware River.
Jacques Lipchitz's sculpture Prometheus Strangling the Vulture *in front of the Philadelphia Museum of Art.*
On the spine: *The Liberty Bell*

Above: *A statue of George Washington stands at Eakins Circle, looking down Benjamin Franklin Parkway toward City Hall. At the other end of the parkway is the Philadelphia Museum of Art.*

Facing page: *Viewed down Broad Street at dusk, City Hall's impressive architecture is on full display. This National Historic Landmark was built between 1871 and 1901, and it is the tallest masonry building in the world. It was the tallest building in Philadelphia until 1987, thanks to an unwritten agreement among city developers.*

Far left: *One of Philadelphia's most famous fictional sons is honored at the top of the steps of the Museum of Art: the footprints of Rocky Balboa from the Sylvester Stallone movie* Rocky.

Left: *A real-life hero to many Philadelphians was former mayor Frank Rizzo, who served for two terms, from 1972 to 1980.*

Above: *Several buildings in downtown Philly now dwarf the City Hall tower.*

Facing page: *Standing 945 feet tall, One Liberty Place usurped City Hall as Philadelphia's tallest building in 1987. The companion building, at Two Liberty Place, was built five years later, measuring in at 848 feet.*

Above: *Philip Syng Physick, considered the father of American surgery, lived and worked in this Society Hill home from 1815 to 1837. It was built in 1786 by wealthy wine importer Henry Hill, who died during a yellow fever epidemic in 1798.*

Right: *St. Peter's Episcopal Church in Society Hill dates back to 1758, though the wooden steeple was added in the 1840s.*

Facing page: *Delancey Street is a tree-lined lane in Society Hill featuring numerous historic homes. The Society Hill district retains many of its original eighteenth- and nineteenth-century brick residences, thanks to preservation efforts begun in the 1950s. It was originally named for the Free Society of Traders, an organization established by William Penn in 1683 to foster commercial development in the young colony.*

The City Tavern first opened its doors in 1774 and included among its patrons such luminaries as Benjamin Franklin, George Washington, Thomas Jefferson, John Adams, and Paul Revere. It was a popular gathering place during the Continental Congresses. The original building was destroyed in 1854 and was reconstructed for the Bicentennial Celebration in 1976. It remains a fashionable eating establishment and watering hole today.

Head House Square in Society Hill was the site of an eighteenth-century marketplace and the Head House Tavern across the street.

Above: Quince Street is one of old Philadelphia's charming and well-kept historic lanes.

Overleaf: Elfreth's Alley is the oldest continually occupied residential street in the United States. A National Historic Landmark, the alley was developed in 1702, and the oldest extant houses date to the 1720s.

Above: *The Independence Seaport Museum at Penn's Landing offers many opportunities to explore the city's rich maritime legacy. You can view boat building or tour historic ships, from the 1892 USS* Olympia *to the World War II submarine, the USS* Becuna.

Facing page: *Second Street and Chestnut in the heart of the Old City is the site of the former Corn Exchange Bank.*

Above: *The Assembly Room at Independence Hall has been restored to its late-eighteenth century appearance, including the chair that George Washington used while presiding over the Constitutional Convention. The original furnishings were used as firewood by British troops occupying the building in the winter of 1777–1778.*

Left: *Free from the footprints of thousands of tourists, Independence Hall is quiet during a winter snowstorm. The centerpiece of Independence National Historical Park, the hall is where the Declaration of Independence was signed on July 4, 1776, and where the United States Constitution was drafted eleven years later. George Washington was appointed commander-in-chief of the Continental Army here in 1775, and the design for the American flag was unveiled in the hall as well.*

Above: *A symbol of America's struggle for independence, the Liberty Bell is now housed in its own pavilion near Independence Hall. The bell was cast in 1752 and recast in 1753. It rang for the last time in 1846, in honor of George Washington's birthday, when its now-famous crack was formed.*

Right: *Construction on Independence Hall began in 1732 and was completed in 1756. At the time it was the State House of the Province of Pennsylvania. The octagonal steeple atop the brick tower was the original location of the Liberty Bell.*

Left: *Gloria Dei, or Old Swedes, Church is the oldest church in Pennsylvania, consecrated in 1700. It is located in Queens Village, which was the site of the old Swedish settlement known as Wicaco. Originally a Swedish Lutheran church, it became part of the Episcopal Church in 1845.*

Below: *The restored interior of Gloria Dei includes models of two ships,* Kalmar Nyckel *and* Fogel Grip, *that brought Swedish settlers to the region in the 1640s.*

The Betsy Ross House is another popular historical attraction in the Old City. Ross lived here from 1773 to 1786. The building was saved from disrepair by school children who collected change to fund the restoration of the national shrine in the early twentieth century.

Left: *The Continental Congress resolved on June 14, 1777, to adopt Ross's design as the official flag of the new nation. Re-enactments of Ross creating the flag take place at the house every Fourth of July.*

Below: *Visitors leave pennies on the gravestone of Benjamin Franklin, the man who wrote, "A penny saved is a penny earned." Franklin is one of five signers of the Declaration of Independence buried at the Christ Church Cemetery in Old City.*

The majestic
Philadelphia
Museum of Art
sits above the old
Fairmount Water
Works on the
banks of the
Schuylkill River.

The Fairmount Water Works delivered clean water to the city of Philadelphia from the 1820s until about 1910. It was one of the first municipal water works in the country, and its waterwheels were a marvel of technology, pumping water from the river to nearby reservoirs.

Above: *The Philadelphia Museum of Art houses more than 300,000 works of art from diverse eras and countries and in various media. It is a grand space inside and out, situated in sprawling Fairmount Park.*

Left: *Edgar Degas's sculpture* The Little Dancer Aged Fourteen *is among the many fine pieces in the Museum of Art's collection.*

More than a dozen statues are on display outside the Museum of Art and through-out Fairmount Park. The Lion Fighter *by Albert Wolff has graced the steps of the museum since 1929.*

Left: *Thorfinn Karlsefni, represented in bronze by Einar Jonsson on Kelly Drive along the Schuylkill River, led an Icelandic expedition to North America in the eleventh century.*

Below: *Frederic Remington's bronze* Cowboy *basks in the golden sunlight on Kelly Drive in Fairmount Park. This large-scale sculpture was Remington's final work.*

Above: *Lovely Fairmount Park covers more than 4,000 acres on both banks of the Schuylkill and is the nation's largest urban park. The city purchased the land in the 1840s to preserve it as a natural area and protect the river from pollution. Today, the park features miles of paths for biking, strolling, or horseback riding; picnic areas; an outdoor amphitheater; historic buildings; a zoo; and acres of gardens and tree stands.*

Facing page: *The Beaux-Arts–style Memorial Hall, on the west bank of the river, was constructed as the centerpiece of the city's 1876 Centennial Exhibition, at a cost of more than $1.5 million. After the exhibition, it served as the home of the Philadelphia Museum of Art for fifty years.*

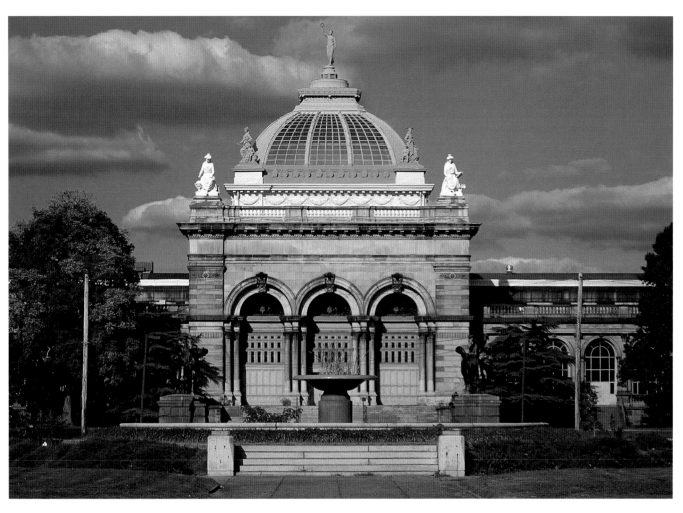

Boathouse Row, here reflected in the Schuylkill River at night, is one of Fairmount Park's premier attractions. Most of the houses were built by boating clubs between 1860 and the early 1880s.

Rich oranges and yellows come to Fairmount Park in autumn, with year-round views of downtown Philadelphia.

When William Penn and his surveyor, Thomas Holme, laid out a plan for the city of Philadelphia in 1682, they created five open squares as public green spaces. Rittenhouse Square remains a lovely neighborhood park for relaxing and people-watching. It is the site of outdoor markets and free concerts in summer as well.

Rittenhouse Square is a place for family fun during winter snowstorms when the city takes on a sleepy white beauty.

Summertime fun can be had in another of William Penn's five open squares: Logan Square. The Swann Memorial Fountain, designed by sculptor Alexander Stirling Calder, is a popular wading pool during the hot, humid summer months.

A longstanding Philadelphia tradition, the girls of John W. Hallahan Catholic High School frolic in the waters of the Logan Square fountain on the last day of school.

Logan Square was redesigned as a circle when Benjamin Franklin Parkway was developed in 1919, and it marked the midway point along the diagonal boulevard extending from Center City to the Museum of Art. Calder's fountain features three bronze Native American figures representing the city's principal waterways. This male warrior represents the Delaware River.

Right: *The grand, rounded portico of the Philadelphia Merchant's Exchange was designed by local architect William Strickland, who also created the design for the Parthenon-inspired national bank building. It is the oldest standing stock exchange building in the country.*

Below: *Down the street from Independence Hall, the Second Bank of the United States operated in this Greek Revival building from 1824 until the bank's charter lapsed in 1836. The building subsequently served as a customs house (1845–1935) and today is a gallery of colonial- and federal-era portraits.*

Left: *The historic, nineteenth-century Bergdoll Mansion and Carriage House is home to the Settlement Music School's West Philadelphia Branch.*

Below: *The Union League of Philadelphia is a private club founded in 1862 that includes some 3,000 members. The League House, covering a full city block, was built in 1865.*

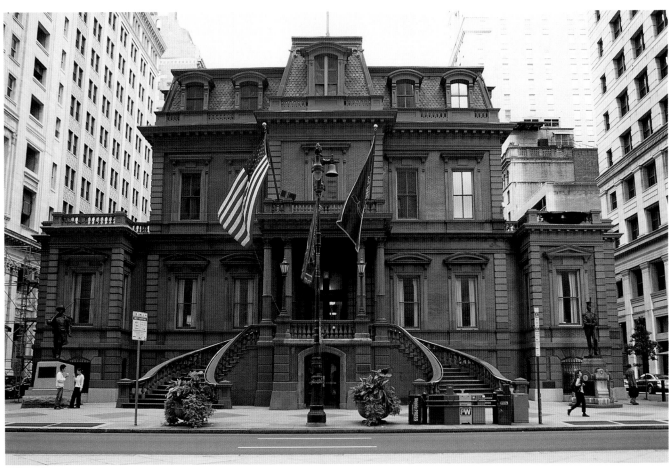

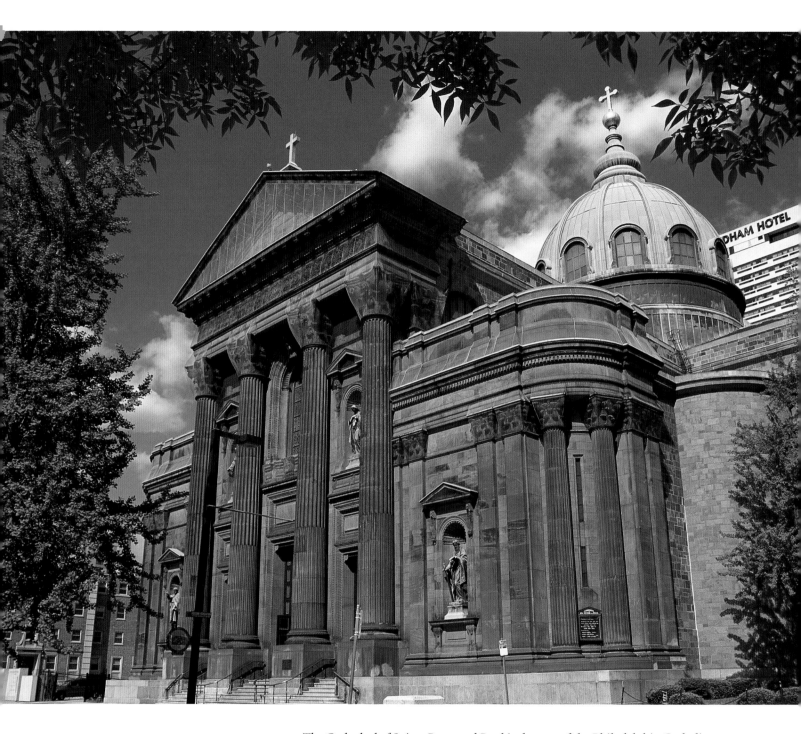

The Cathedral of Saints Peter and Paul is the seat of the Philadelphia Catholic Archdiocese. Completed in 1864 across from Logan Square, the Italian Renaissance–style church was modeled after the churches of Rome.

Above: *The Eastern State Penitentiary opened in 1829 as a model of prison reform and influenced prison construction throughout the world. During its 142 years of operation, it housed notorious criminals such as Al Capone. It is open for tours today.*

Left: *The Mütter Museum at the College of Physicians of Philadelphia displays a large collection of medical artifacts and curiosities, from the Chevalier Jackson Collection of objects swallowed and removed, to complete skeletons of a midget and a giant.*

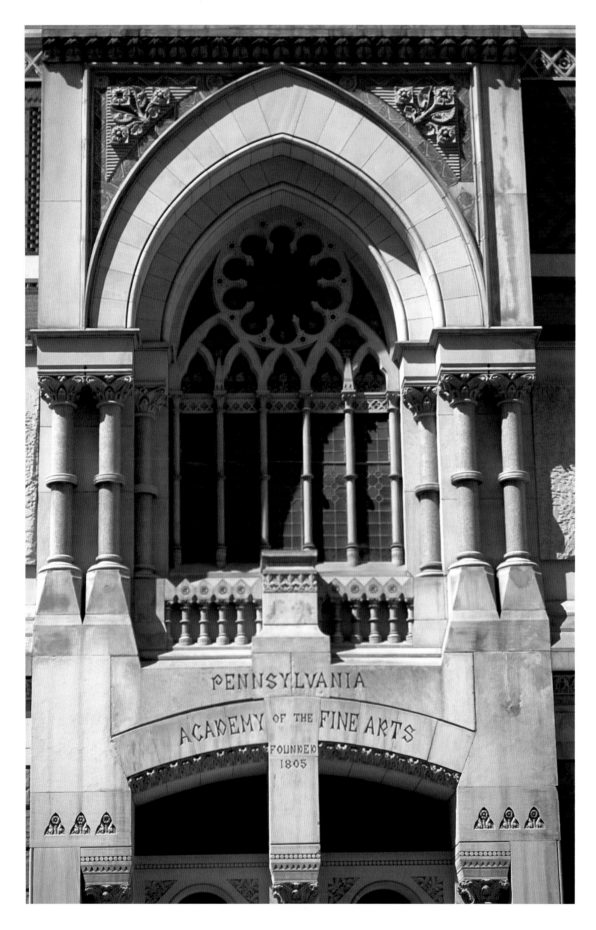

Founded in 1805, the Pennsylvania Academy of Fine Arts is the oldest museum in the United States. The museum holds an impressive collection of American paintings, sculpture, and other works, and its School of Fine Arts is a premier institution. The academy moved to its current location, a National Historic Landmark on North Broad Street, in 1876.

The Academy of Music, built in 1857, remains one of the grandest halls in the United States. The elegant 2,900-seat main hall has been the venue for American premieres of many noted operas, performed by the Opera Company of Philadelphia.

Above: *Within the Kimmel Center's glass-covered atrium, the 2,500-seat Verizon Hall serves as the Philadelphia Orchestra's main venue. The 650-seat Perelman Theater accommodates smaller ensembles and recitals.*

Left: *Along with the Academy of Music, the Merriam Theater, and the University of the Arts, the Kimmel Center for the Performing Arts is located in the heart of the "Avenue of the Arts" along Broad Street. The Kimmel Center opened in 2001 as the new home for the Philadelphia Orchestra.*

Above: *The nearly 20,000 students enrolled at Penn's four undergraduate and twelve graduate schools attend classes in striking Gothic buildings such as this.*

Right: *The towers of the Quadrangle have been welcoming students to the University of Pennsylvania in West Philadelphia since 1895. Founded in 1751, Penn was the nation's first liberal arts college focused on preparing students for business and public service.*

Above: *Benjamin Franklin, one of the University of Pennsylvania's founders, is represented in several statues on the Penn campus. Here he enjoys the company of a bronze pigeon and a real-life squirrel.*

Right: *A couple of Philadelphians find time to relax on a bench in a South Philly park.*

The streets of South Philadelphia, one of the city's oldest districts, are lined with row houses. Prime parking spaces in this lively residential neighborhood are often guarded like Fort Knox!

Antique lovers are drawn to Antique Row along Pine Street between Ninth and Twelfth Streets. Many of its shops go back generations.

One of the many quaint shops on Antique Row, Kohn & Kohn Antiques has been selling furniture, stained glass, artwork, and more since the 1930s.

Twentieth Street in the Rittenhouse Square neighborhood is another good spot to shop for unique bargains.

South Street has a flair all its own. In addition to the many colorful shops, you will often find off-beat parades heading along the thoroughfare. The street formed the southern boundary of the city in early colonial times.

Above:
This old synagogue in the South Street District is now an indoor antiques market.

Right: *The cornucopia of establishments on South Street offers something for everyone.*

Facing page: *Congregation B'Nai Abraham is an active synagogue on Lombard Street, one block north of South Street. Many Jewish immigrants from Eastern Europe settled in South Philadelphia during the late nineteenth and early twentieth centuries.*

The KNAVE of HEARTS

RESTAURANT & BAR

922 3956

Est. 1975

MAGAZINES
CIGARETTES
Cranky's
HANDBAGS
COLD DRINKS

Right: *This uniquely decorated door in North Philadelphia reflects its owner's creative flair.*

Below: *Several buildings in the South Street area are imaginatively decorated with glass and tile mosaics, many by the same artist.*

Many North Philadelphia row houses have been updated for a contemporary look, though the neighborhood experienced its biggest boom in the late nineteenth century. Today it is a diverse neighborhood, with a growing Latino population in eastern North Philly.

Ile-Ife Park is a community garden in North Philadelphia featuring sculptures, murals, and mosaics. It was initiated in 1986 by artist Lily Yeh as part of an effort to revitalize the area's vacant lots as safe and appealing public spaces. Ile-Ife Park was the inaugural project of a nonprofit organization called the Village of Arts and Humanities.

Left: *At Thomas Alva Edison/John C. Fareira High School in North Philadelphia, an art project commemorates former students who lost their lives in the Vietnam War. More former Edison students died in the war than from any other high school in the country.*

Philadelphia's parks and playgrounds provide ample opportunities for childhood fun and games.

Right: *Colorful murals adorn playgrounds and other spaces throughout the city, many of them celebrating Philadelphia's multicultural heritage.*

Below and facing page: *Established in 1984 as the Anti-Graffiti Network, Philadelphia's Mural Arts Program has enlivened the cityscape. This mural, entitled* Common Threads, *was designed by artist Meg Fish Saligman and is the largest mural in the city. It is located at the intersection of Broad and Spring Garden Streets.*

The Mural Arts Program has been more prolific than any other public arts program in the country, creating over 2,400 murals throughout the city.

Above: *South Philly still reflects its longstanding Italian heritage, with church festivals and other cultural events held throughout the year.*

Left: *A portrait of former mayor Frank Rizzo looms large over South Philadelphia's Ninth Street Italian Market. It is the oldest and largest working outdoor market in the United States.*

Above: *Nothing says Philadelphia quite like one of the city's famous cheese steak sandwiches. Geno's Steaks is a South Philly institution, open twenty-four hours a day, seven days a week. Pat's King of Steaks, located right across the street from Geno's, is another leading contender for best Philly cheese steak.*

Left: *The Di Bruno Brothers market has been selling fine cheeses, gourmet meats, and a wide variety of olives and other specialties since 1939. Located in the heart of the Ninth Street Italian Market, it remains a family business, now run by grandsons of one of the founding Di Brunos.*

Right: *This Amish girl made the fifty-mile trip from Lancaster County to work Philadelphia's Reading Terminal Market. The terminal, once the largest train shed in the world, now accommodates more than eighty merchants selling food, clothing, crafts, and other goods from around the world.*

Below: *Rittenhouse Square also hosts a busy outdoor market that attracts growers and merchants from throughout the metropolitan area.*

Originally an industrial area of factories and mills, Manayunk is now a chic shopping and dining district. It is located north of the city on the east bank of the Schuylkill River. The name Manayunk comes from a Lenni Lenape Indian word meaning "where we go to drink"—though probably not in reference to the area's numerous bars and night clubs.

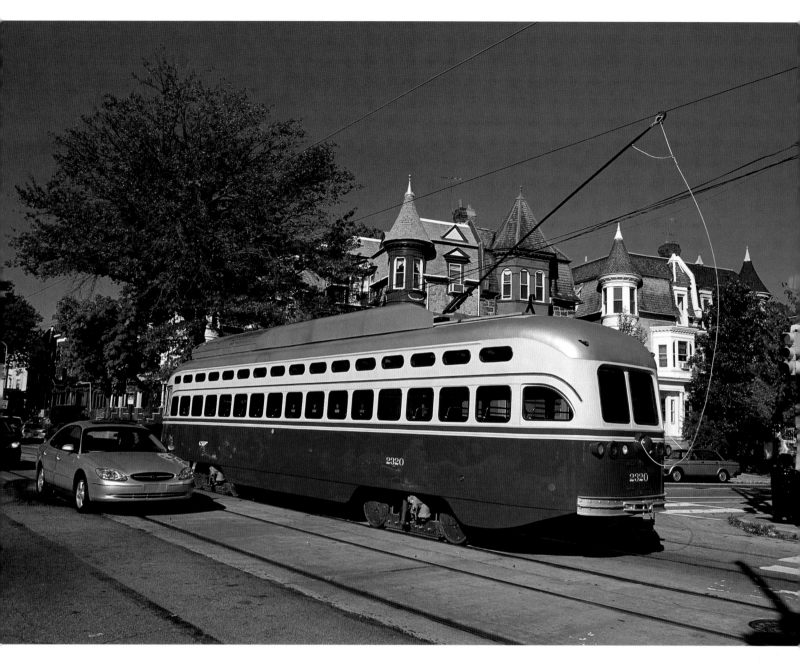

Philadelphia once had an extensive trolley system to transport residents around the city. Several lines have been brought back into service, such as this 1940s-era streetcar rolling through West Philadelphia.

West Philadelphia is a diverse neighborhood across the Schuylkill from Center City. This castle-like residence demonstrates the area's varied architecture.

Squirrel Hill Falls Park was designed by Danielle Rousseau-Hunter as a public performance space, although questions over its funding and use created some controversy.

The historic Old City district offers an array of dining and entertainment options.

Left: *Philadelphia's proud Irish community comes out in full force for the annual St. Patrick's Day Parade.*

Below: *Fergie's Pub on Sansom Street is a classic Irish pub and a fine place for a refreshing pint.*

Polish-American girls dress in the attire of their ancestral land during the Polish Festival held at the Our Lady of Czestochowa Shrine near Doylestown.

Herding geese across Broad Street in Center City is an annual tradition at the Von Steuben Day Parade, a celebration of German heritage held every autumn.

Far left: *African and African-American heritage and culture is celebrated during the Odunde Festival, featuring dancers, musicians, and various other activities.*

Left: *The region's Indian community also comes together for an annual festival at Penn's Landing, providing an opportunity to explore the traditions and cuisine of this south Asian nation.*

Above: *Mexican Independence Day is commemorated in a lively gathering at Penn's Landing every fall.*

Facing page: *The Puerto Rican Festival, culminating in the Puerto Rican Day Parade, is one of many cultural events held during the summer and early fall. Here the festival queen rides down Benjamin Franklin Parkway toward City Hall in her place of honor.*

Philadelphia's bustling Chinatown is marked by the Friendship Gate at Tenth and Arch Streets. The growing community, located just west of Old City, has been a focal point for Chinese immigrants coming to Philadelphia since the nineteenth century.

Left: *Chinatown features dozens of restaurants and grocery stores offering fine Chinese delicacies.*

Below: *Chinese New Year is cause for grand celebration in Chinatown, complete with music, firecrackers, and elaborate costumes.*

Right: *Sequins, feathers, and vibrant colors are the order of the day at the Mummers Parade. Participants often begin work on their costumes a year ahead of time, and at great expense.*

Below: *Every New Year's Day, thousands of outrageously dressed "Mummers" parade through Center City. The Mummers tradition in Philadelphia goes back to colonial times, but the first official, city-sanctioned parade was held in 1901.*

Left: *Crowds pack the sidewalks on chilly New Year's mornings to watch the creative concoctions strolling by.*

Below: *Costumed and choreographed string bands bring up the rear at the Mummers Parade, following the Comics and the Fancies. The bands can also be seen performing in the city year round.*

The Peoplehood Parade, "An All-City Parade and Pageant," is a celebration of community and social justice organized by the Spiral Q Puppet Theater every October.

The Spiral Q Puppet Theater was established in the late 1990s as a forum for addressing the needs and concerns of Philadelphia's diverse urban communities. In addition to the citywide Peoplehood Parade, Spiral Q works with neighborhood partners to organize pageants and parades on a local level.

Above: *Mayor John Street leads the city's fashionable Easter Promenade up South Street.*

Facing page: *Philadelphia's big Fourth of July parade features large floats by day and exquisite fireworks displays by night.*

Right: *Philadelphians love their bicycles and show up in numbers for rallies and races.*

Below: *The ten-kilometer Rocky Run attracts runners from throughout the greater Philadelphia area, so it may require some extra effort to stand out in the crowd.*

"Double-Dutch" jump roping originated in the playgrounds of Philadelphia, and competitions bring together the best double-Dutch teams from around the region.

The Philadelphia Eagles inaugurated brand-new Lincoln Financial Field for the 2004 National Football League season. The 68,500-seat state-of-the-art facility cost more than $500 million to construct.

The Eagles won their first seven games at Lincoln Financial, including a 30-8 drubbing of the Carolina Panthers early in the 2004 campaign.

Philadelphia's baseball team also got a new stadium in 2004, replacing the indistinctive Veterans Stadium with the more charming and inviting Citizens Bank Park. The intimate retro-styled ballpark was built exclusively for baseball, and the Phillies drew good crowds in 2004.

The six-foot-six-inch-tall Phillie Phanatic has been entertaining Philadelphia baseball crowds since 1978.

Above, both photos: *The Penn Relays is the nation's oldest and largest track-and-field meet for high school and college athletes. The three-day event is held every spring at the University of Pennsylvania's Franklin Field.*

Right: *The Dad Vail Regatta is the oldest competition of its kind in the country. Thousands of student athletes descend on Philadelphia during the second week of May to participate in this foremost collegiate rowing competition.*

Like an Eakins painting, a scene of sculling on the Schuylkill is timeless.

Plans to build a bridge across the Delaware River from Philadelphia to Camden, New Jersey, were proposed as early as 1818, but it didn't come to pass until 1926, when the Benjamin Franklin Bridge opened. In addition to seven lanes of automobile traffic, the bridge has two outer lanes for rapid transit train tracks.

Above, top: *The Benjamin Franklin Bridge was open only to foot traffic and classic cars on display for the bridge's seventy-fifth anniversary celebration in 2001.*

Above, bottom: *Amtrak's Acela Express bullet train leaves from Philadelphia's Thirtieth Street Station on its way between New York City and Washington, D.C.*

The art deco Penn Center Suburban Station was once the city's main railway terminal, but today most trains coming into Philadelphia from locations far and wide go only as far as the Thirtieth Street Station. Suburban Station now serves mostly commuter lines.

Originally called Pennsylvania Station, the grand Thirtieth Street Station was built as part of the same transportation improvement project that created Suburban Station in Center City during the early 1930s. The Thirtieth Street Station is one of the busiest train terminals in the United States.

Philadelphia's Main Line is famous for its stately homes. The term "Main Line" came from the area's proximity to the Pennsylvania Railroad's main line. Many Victorian-era train stations continue to serve the communities along the railway.

General George Washington and his Continental Army spent a brutal winter encamped at Valley Forge across the Schuylkill from Philadelphia in 1777–1778. Even under a thick blanket of snow, the site is a much more comfortable place to visit today, within the Valley Forge National Historic Park.

Above: *Among the Valley Forge site's historic buildings is the Isaac Potts House, which served as General Washington's headquarters at the encampment.*

Left: *John Bartram was a pioneering eighteenth-century American botanist and naturalist, and his forty-five-acre home site is now a National Historic Landmark open to the public. Historic Bartram's Garden is in West Philadelphia on the Schuylkill River.*

Now a neighborhood within the city of Philadelphia, Germantown was first settled as a separate community by German immigrants in the late seventeenth century.

Left: *Children dressed in the garb of early colonial settlers are on hand for the re-creation of the Battle of Germantown.*

Below: *The 1777 Battle of Germantown was a pivotal event in the Revolutionary War. Although British troops thwarted Washington's offensive, the near victory by the Continental Army served to lift morale and rallied support for the cause. This monumental battle is re-created at the site every year.*

George Washington leading a ragtag army across the Delaware River on December 25, 1776, to wage a battle on the Hessian garrison at Trenton, New Jersey, was a landmark moment in the war for independence. Washington Crossing Historic Park, about forty-five minutes from Center City Philadelphia, commemorates this event with a re-enactment every Christmas Day.